SPEAK TO *ME*

SPEAK TO *ME*

J. H. C. GREEN

THE ODYSSEY PRESS
The Bobbs-Merrill Company, Inc., Publishers
Indianapolis · New York

© COPYRIGHT, 1962
BY THE ODYSSEY PRESS, INC.

The Odyssey Press
A Division of The Bobbs-Merrill Company, Inc.
Printed in the United States of America
Library of Congress Catalog Card Number: 62-14943
ISBN 0-672-63116-4(pbk)
Seventh Printing

PREFACE

The purpose of this book is to help two large groups of people: those who are scared to death of getting up on their feet to make a talk and those who feel that only the greatly blessed can do this adequately.

To the first group, I speak from the heart. As a young man I had every advantage, yet as president of my senior class in high school and captain of the baseball team, I was filled with a dread amounting to terror of the necessary little public talks. In college and in a dozen years of business, though I got along well with people, I avoided as I would the plague anything resembling a public speech. After graduating as an officer candidate in World War II, I was startled to be assigned back to the Infantry School as a weapons instructor. The first time I confronted two hundred candidates with a fifty minute memorized lecture on the intricacies of the 37 mm. gun drill, I barely made it through, leaving the gun crew horrified with the gun still pointing at the sky, where it had no business being. From the humiliation of that moment grew a vigorous determination to get this fear off my back. May I say, not as a boast, but to give hope to the fearful, that when I left instructional duties three years later, I went with two promotions, an extremely high efficiency rating, and a letter saying that in one well-placed man's opinion I was one of the three best instructors in the history of the Infantry School. I was invited to try college teaching after I left the service, and for the last fourteen years I have been teaching, of all things, Public Speaking! In all seriousness, if I can beat this particular fear, you can too.

To the second group, may I say that the gifted have no monopoly on common sense, compassion, cooperation, justice, initiative, and other qualities that affect human relations and our daily lives. It is my opinion backed by experience that any man who has an idea or a feeling can learn with a little determination to present his position acceptably. You in all probability will not become a second Winston Churchill, very true. But there is nothing the least bit mysterious in the planning, the preparation, and the delivery of an adequate little talk. No matter what your field, your position in the field, your age, your sex, you can learn to do some justice to your ideas and to your feelings. You can learn by yourself, but probably better in a group or in a class, but you *can* learn. Go ahead and try.

Obviously this is not, and is not meant to be, a definitive, all inclusive text on public speaking. Its purpose is to help the thousands of people who need help in this area, and to help them in a simple, clear, easy way. To those of you who read the material in this book, let me add a word of good cheer—it works!

J. H. C. GREEN

Auburn, Alabama

CONTENTS

Preface	vii
Chapter 1 Scared?	1
Chapter 2 Speak to *Me*	10
Chapter 3 Two Speaking Situations	23
Chapter 4 Build the Talk Carefully	29
Chapter 5 The Introduction	36
Chapter 6 The Body	44
Chapter 7 The Finishing Touches	54
Chapter 8 "By Sweetness"	61
Chapter 9 May I Present?	67
Chapter 10 Learn Together	70

SPEAK TO *ME*

CHAPTER 1

SCARED?

I start my beginning public speaking classes by asking for written, unsigned replies to the following question, "What is your attitude toward getting up on your feet and talking to a group?" The answers may surprise you.

Three out of every four students say they feel real fear of this situation. There are such comments as "scared to death," "just hope I can do it," "my hands and feet turn cold at the thought of it." Furthermore, one third of these people say they have avoided the course as long as they possibly could, putting it off till senior year and often till the very quarter in which they graduate, instead of taking it at the normal time, which is the end of their freshman year or the beginning of their sophomore year. Obviously at this stage of the game, these normal, active, intelligent, young Americans take no pleasure in the thought of standing before a group and talking. To show that they qualify for the above adjectives, let me give you a quick rundown of the people in one typical class. In this group there are three students who belong to academic honor societies, the presidents of a fraternity, a sorority, and an English club, a miler, two halfbacks, a 250-pound tackle and his pal, a 125-pound wrestler, a catcher, a Navy veteran, four married men, one married woman, two sorority girls, a senior in engineering physics, and a senior in premedicine. This is a good cross section of college students, and I think it is fair to assume that if most of these people are disturbed at the thought of talking in public, many, many others are too. Actually, my little surveys are pretty much in line with explorations made on a much broader front.

There is no argument that fear, or call it stage fright if you will, is a problem for a large number of beginners in public speaking. Fear is so widespread that it is entirely accepted by the experienced instructor, but unfortunately not many other people understand it. The average beginner who feels fear tends to believe he is a freak, to think there is something wrong with him. He believes this problem is his alone. Let me assure you this simply is not true. No one has a monopoly on stage fright. And no one need feel guilty or ashamed about it. It is a commonplace, natural reaction to a disturbing situation, and it most certainly can be cut down to acceptable size.

It is interesting, I believe, to note that many people, able and competent in other fields, feel this same fear when first drawn into public speaking. For instance, a football coach whose name you would recognize told me that when he first became head coach he would pace the floor of his hotel room, not before a game but before addressing any alumni group. He is now a polished speaker with no fear apparent to the public eye. Some years ago a top-ranking tennis player told me he loved to win a tournament but dreaded the little talk he had to make later in accepting the trophy. He now is a highly successful salesman. An infantry officer decorated three times in World War II would go to any extreme to avoid making a talk. Now he is a steadily re-elected politician to whom a speech is routine. And so it goes. Perhaps by now you can see that stage fright is not the usual fear of physical things that can hurt you, such as a tornado, a machine gun, a snake, the dentist's drill. You need courage to face these things, but if we define courage as the ability to meet danger with firmness, where is the danger in the public speaking situation? Obviously, there is none. What, then, are we afraid of? Let's face it. We are afraid of ourselves. We are afraid that what we say, or what we do, or how we look may give the group a lower opinion of us. As the boys would say, we are afraid of goofing off in front of all present.

Now that we have pinned down the problem, let's see what can be done toward a solution. First of all, the basic defense against stage fright is to select a purpose that is meaningful to you and to prepare thoroughly for your talk. If you are talking about something close to your heart or to your mind and if you are well prepared, what is there to fear? On the other hand, if you are poorly prepared, it is hard to keep fear out, and justly so, because you know you are likely to do badly and you probably will. Much of this book is an attempt to show you how to get ready.

In addition to being prepared, you can help yourself by understanding and accepting some ideas about stage fright. First of all, you must believe as we have pointed out before that you are no freak to feel this fear. You have a great deal of company. There is no need to feel guilty or ashamed.

Second, please accept the idea that, even though you feel this fear strongly, you can walk and you can talk and you can move your hands. Of the hundreds and hundreds of students I have had, only one boy could not function, and he was really a clinical case. It developed that he had a tremendous burden of guilt from a war experience which left him sure that everyone who looked at him knew he was a coward. He could talk to me alone, and gradually he could continue as a man or two was added to the group. On the last day, he talked to the whole group. He was sweating like a horse, but he did it. Now, years later, he writes that he has made a good bit of money. How? Selling prefab houses and real estate. So even that lone exception had a happy ending. You'll find that your mind and voice and body can operate pretty well in spite of stage fright. You can function.

Third, I offer you an idea that is very difficult for most beginners to accept, but it is true. You just don't look as nervous or as frightened as you feel. Honestly, you don't. Your inner turmoil is not revealed for everyone to see. Let me give you one typical example out of scores available. A girl once came to my office to tell me she was simply terrified over her first talk, which she was to make later that day. She was sure everyone would know how afraid she was. But in the talk her delivery was pleasant, clear, and lively. She used gestures and was as animated as she would be in a conversation. There certainly was no sign of turmoil visible to me or to the class, yet the girl found this hard to believe. The class, on the other hand, found it hard to believe that she was as frightened as she said she was. She had poise, which can be called grace under pressure, and, surprisingly enough, many beginning speakers have it. Some do not, of course, but even they do not show their tension as much as they think they do. Beginning speakers seem particularly worried about three ways they think they reveal tension.

For instance, they worry about getting red in the face as they talk, but this can be the result of an earnest, vigorous delivery and is quite commonplace. It takes about ten thousand times as much energy to send a voice loud and clear to the back of the room as it does to whisper. Consequently, the man who talks with enthusiasm and vigor will use up energy just as he will doing actual physical work. Therefore, it is quite natural for increased color to appear in his face. To this day, my face stays pink for a good half-hour after I've talked, and on the days when I talk three hours in a row I am more tired afterwards than I am after playing eighteen holes of golf. Vigorous talk takes energy so both these results are perfectly natural.

In addition, the beginner often thinks his voice is quavering. Occasionally, this is true, but much more often it is not. The ear and the so-called mechanism by which we make sound are so closely placed that it is often difficult for the speaker to appraise his voice accurately. The supersensitive beginner believes that he hears something no one else hears. Scores of beginners have asked me, "Was my voice shaking, Prof?" And almost without exception I have told them, "No, I didn't notice and I doubt that anyone else did. Stop worrying about it."

Another concern which is more valid than the others is that the beginner's hands may tremble. There are some things to do about this which may surprise you. First, don't try to control it. That will only increase the muscle tension and make the shaking worse. But the muscles may relax with a little work, so try to move your body. Take a few steps from one side of the lectern to the other. Try to let yourself go enough to make a few gestures. As the football players say after one of them gets a knock that hurts, "Shake it off." Or if you prefer, just go ahead and call the attention of the audience to your hands. The response is invariably amused but sympathetic. And you will learn what experienced speakers know, that audiences are almost always friendly. A little later you will probably be surprised to notice your hands are no longer trembling. Here, as in all other aspects of stage fright, good preparation is a big help.

Another thought, which I hope you will accept, is that you will almost certainly gain confidence with speaking experience. The more you expose yourself to speaking situations, the more you find that you can handle them successfully. This requires a certain amount of determination. You have to force yourself into what is at first an unpleasant situation, but, if you continue, much of the unpleasantness drops away. It is surprising how many people who have the will to go through with a definite speaking program actually come to enjoy standing up and speaking to a group. This, too, is hard for many people to believe, but here again could I give scores of examples. At the conclusion of the beginning Public Speaking course, boy after boy has said to me, "I thought it would never happen, but I actually like this." This speaking business differs very little from other realms of social experience. Thousands and thousands of Americans have been fearful about whether or not they could dance well enough to go to a party, or would dress properly for a certain social function, or know which fork to use at a formal dinner, etc., and yet the original fear that all these people have disappears as they become better acquainted with the situation and learn enough and have enough experience to be confident they can handle it. Much the same way with public speaking—a little learning and a little experience and soon, instead of a great deal of fear, there is some confidence. And with more experience comes more confidence.

Before your talk you will naturally want to take pains with your appearance. At the risk of seeming to belabor the obvious, may I point out that the clean shave, the fresh shirt, the well-tied tie, the pressed suit will all contribute to your sense of well-being. The problem of appearance, of course, also faces the woman who speaks. No mere man, at least not this one, would be bold enough to prescribe the perfect costume. The idea, in my opinion, is to look pleasant and acceptable. The extreme in dress and make-up, the too-too weird hat, can cause quite an effect, but often at the expense of the speech. No excuse should be given for a quiet or perhaps not so quiet discussion of your appearance. Again, in my opinion, simplicity and conservatism in appearance furnish the best background for a talk.

For a final bit of encouragement, may I ask you to look at the results of the little survey I make at the end of the Public Speaking course?

The seventy-five percent of the students who confessed marked fear at the beginning of the course have now dropped to only seven percent, a rather startling reduction.

At the start only five percent thought they had any ability to communicate in a public speaking situation. Here, by our widespread use of the term "a speech," I believe we have unwittingly set up quite a hurdle for beginners, causing the average man and the average student to think of a speech as a major address such as Mr. Stevenson might give before the U.N. Quite naturally he doubts his ability to handle it. Often, at the beginning of the course, when I ask a boy if he thinks he can make a *speech* about his home town, he will answer in the negative. But if I ask him to make a little talk about his home town, he will agree every time. The connotations of the words are indeed different. Any normal person can learn to make the clear, interesting, effective little talk that he will need and use in his sphere of life. One day the talk may grow into quite a speech, but for now, let's leave the idea of a major speech to the debaters and to those in the advanced courses. My students seem to accept this concept readily because at the end of the course over seventy percent of them, instead of five percent, feel that they can communicate fairly well with a group.

The next figure is interesting, too. At the beginning only seven percent say they think they will enjoy talking to a group. At the end, almost seventy-five percent say they do enjoy it. May I suggest that you study these figures a little?

I don't take the extreme position that a course in public speaking will cure all of a man's problems, but I do feel that it can result in some dramatic changes in attitude and performance. The reason I have kept on teaching the beginning course for so many years is that I believe no other course helps so many people so much. Now let's get down to the business of preparing and delivering a talk.

CHAPTER 2

SPEAK TO *ME*

THE DELIVERY

Delivery is the effort of a speaker to communicate his thoughts to the audience. It consists of his sounds, movements, and expressions in front of the group. It is futile to argue which is more important, good delivery or good content. Obviously a speech has no value unless the speaker has something to say, no matter how well he says nothing. And just as obviously the speech, no matter how fine the content, is worthless if the words of the speaker cannot be heard or understood.

In conversation, many people are lively and vigorous. They look at the person spoken to. Facial expression and gestures help them convey their meaning, especially where feeling is involved. They are well on the way to good delivery. Yet these same people, involved in a beginning public speaking situation, will often turn to stone. I've seen it happen a thousand times at the beginning of the course. With some, fear is so strong that they cannot talk conversationally until they see that they can function in spite of fear. Others, I believe, are inhibited by the false idea that they have to be something other than themselves in front of the group. Ironically, the problem in good delivery for many beginners is to keep and use a skill they already have. It is just hard for some people to believe that they can stand up and talk effectively to several seated people in much the same way they talk to friends at the coffee table. But that's what we are after—conversational delivery with a few refinements.

Now let's look at good delivery more closely. It is based, of course, on adequate preparation of the talk. Some natural extroverts can do fairly well without much preparation, but for others the security and confidence which thorough preparation brings cannot be found elsewhere. Nothing can beat it as a defense against stage fright. Then too, for a little added confidence on the day of your talk, make sure your appearance is acceptable.

Before your talk you will be seated in the audience, or on a stage, or at a table. Someone will introduce you to the group. Then, before you start your talk, you have two little problems: first, to move to the speaker's stand, unless you can simply stand and speak where you are; second, to acknowledge the introduction and greet the group. For the first, just walk up as though you belonged there. A little confidence and a little dignity will do it. Watch out for any motion or slouch or exaggeration of speed which might create an unfavorable impression before you have even said a word. Once you are behind the lectern, stand comfortably balanced on both feet. Some people say, "Stand tall." At any rate, you must accept the fact that people are looking at you and stand so as to do yourself justice. The lectern can be a trap. Keep up and away from it. The taller the man, the greater seems to be the tendency to flop on the lectern.

About this time the question usually arises, what do I do with my hands? My advice is not to worry about them. Put them on the lectern, let them hang at your sides, put them behind your back, but beware of getting and staying in one fixed position all through your talk. Remember that you are trying to be as easy and natural as you are in conversation. The habit of putting hands in pockets, which many men have in conversing, is not good though for more than a few moments in front of a group. All too often the temptation to jingle change in a pocket is irresistible, and often it is hard to get a hand out of a pocket smoothly for a gesture.

Now, may I urge you to do one more little thing before you start talking—just keep quiet for a few seconds. It is curious how effective a short pause is in getting attention, and it gives the audience a chance to get set for you.

In every aspect of public speaking, I am a strong believer in courteous simplicity. Therefore, I feel that a simple response to the speaker's introduction and a simple greeting to the audience is in good taste and is sufficient. "Thank you, Mr. Chairman. Ladies and gentlemen," should do these jobs perfectly well. This will vary, of course, with the circumstances, and the appropriate is usually a matter of common sense. "Thank you, Madame Chairman. Members of the Garden Club." "Thank you, Tom Jones. Members of XYZ fraternity," etc. I see nothing accomplished by trying to greet every classification and group which compose the audience. I once heard a man tick off seven categories in his greeting and felt a little hurt because he left mine out. "Ladies and gentlemen" would have suited me better. Very rarely will the average speaker encounter such distinguished people in his audience that the courtesy of naming them will be necessary. Even then, I like it simple. For instance, "Governor Jones, ladies and gentlemen."

With these preliminaries over, you launch into your talk. Let's set up some objectives for you. First of all, try to look at the audience and at different parts of the audience as much as you possibly can. Directness, or eye contact, is vital to good delivery. If the speaker shows interest in the audience by looking at them, the audience will tend to stay interested in the speaker. On the other hand, if the speaker looks long out the window or down at the floor, normal human curiosity makes the audience wonder what in the dickens he sees and they soon lose track of his words. Then, too, as the speaker grows more experienced in looking at the group, he becomes better able to judge how well his talk is being followed. He becomes aware that additions and review may be necessary to clarify one point while another point has obviously been understood perfectly. Many beginning speakers find that good eye contact is easy and natural, but to others it can be a real problem. For instance, a husky youngster who will be a champion wrestler one day looks only at the ceiling. A married man, father of three children, seldom raises his eyes from the lectern. A Navy veteran fixes his eyes on me in the back row and looks nowhere else until his talk is over.

One of the brightest boys in school looks steadily at the part of the audience to his left, never to his right. With awareness and determination these problems will be overcome, and they must be, because directness is absolutely vital to good communication. Ideally every member of the audience should have the feeling that you are looking at him and are often speaking directly to him during the talk.

Another major objective of delivery is to speak loudly enough and clearly enough so that everyone in the group can hear and understand. If the sound waves the speaker makes don't reach the ears of the audience strongly enough to be heard or clearly enough to be recognized, there is no meaning to the talk. It is just a waste of time and effort for all concerned. Yet this should present no problem to the normal healthy person. Just talk with enough force to reach the people in the back row. That takes care of all in between. Very rarely does a speaker talk much too loud. It can be annoying if he does, but at least the voice can be heard and understood, while too soft a sound is completely futile. Usually if you are interested in what you are talking about and want to communicate, volume will pretty well take care of itself. Any normal human being can make all the noise he needs, especially today when microphones and loud speakers are almost always provided for audiences of over one hundred. Occasionally, however, there are people who find it very difficult to believe that they cannot be heard. They seem to assume that there is something wrong with the listeners. In one class it took me a month to convince two girls high on the academic honors list that their beautifully prepared talks were not being heard beyond the first row. And even then I doubt that I would have succeeded without the help of written comments from the members of the class. If people say they can't hear you, believe them. You can turn loose more force or volume. Everyone in the audience is entitled to hear without strain.

A further objective in good delivery is the avoidance of any distracting, repeated mannerism. These are sounds without meaning or movements which sooner or later become annoying, often to the point where the audience loses all interest in the talk. The meaningless sounds, *uh, and-uh, er,* are often heard and are known as vocalized pauses. No one cares about an occasional *uh,* but the constantly repeated vocalized pause can be as maddening as the old Chinese torture of letting a drop of water fall every few seconds on the head of the victim. I once attended a lecture by a man nationally known in his field. I regret that all I remember of it is that he had a low of three *uhs* per minute, a high of twelve and an average of eight. Undoubtedly he was unconscious of this defeating habit, just as most beginners are. And it is pleasant to report that, once these people are made aware of the fault, all those with a little determination can correct it. One further word. Once in a while, a boy will start his talk with a loud and clear *uh.* I always feel that he is checking the mechanism and now, reassured that it is in working condition, can continue with his talk. But it does jolt the audience. Try to avoid the *uh* at that time especially.

Occasionally a man will repeat and emphasize one word so often in a talk that it loses its meaning and has the same status as *uh.* For instance, I often have students who must fight the habit of starting every sentence after their first with the word "and." I remember an able man who used "now" at the beginning of every sentence and phrase, over a hundred times in a rather short talk. This has exactly the same annoying effect on the audience as does the often repeated vocalized pause. One way to avoid both these mistakes is to keep your mouth closed, and I mean literally closed, until you are sure of what you want to say next.

Other sounds such as those from tapping on the lectern, cracking knuckles, or shuffling feet can also annoy the audience. One football center with size fourteen shoes had trouble talking at first without slapping one foot and then the other on the floor as though he were going to break into a buck and wing. Who even tried to listen to the talk with such a rhythmic noise going on?

Chewing gum has won a real place for itself in the American way of life, but that place is not in the mouth of a speaker. There are a lot of horrible examples. For instance, some years ago a boy gave the most fascinating talk I have ever seen. He spoke with vigor, and as he did, part of his wad of gum would slide out and dangle down to his chin. Then with a lightning dart of his long tongue he would retrieve it. The suspense was terrific. Next time would the gum escape? I didn't hear a word he said.

Another major distraction for the audience is the repeated, aimless movement of any part of the body. Here is a beginning speaker who bounces on his heels; another pulls the lobe of his ear; another fools with his belt buckle; another strokes his chin. This type of thing, if repeated often, focuses all audience attention on it, and the words of the talk are lost. It is a very good rule to keep your hands away from your head and face when you are speaking, and this goes for conversation, too.

In contrast, the purposeful, meaningful gesture has a real place in speech. It can add emphasis and clarity and it can also help release tension. At the beginning of a speech course few people are willing to use gestures (meaningful movements of any part of the body) but as they gain confidence and realize that this is not very different from conversation, gestures start to appear. The natural, sincere, vigorous gesture can be very effective. Personally, I prefer them to the more stylized, prettied-up ones. If a man becomes enthusiastic about his topic, any problems in delivery usually disappear. Enthusiasm brings with it directness, vigor, animation, gestures. The speaker forgets about himself in his real desire to communicate with the audience. We do not see nearly enough of this quality in public speaking, because, I feel sure, many speakers pick their topics without asking themselves the question, "Do I feel the least bit enthusiastic about this?" If the answer is no, for their own sake and the sake of the audience they had better look further.

So then good delivery is direct, clear, alive, vigorous. Find enthusiasm and you have it all.

MAKING KNOWN SOUNDS

Because we have already seen that one of the problems in delivery centers around the ability to make sounds loudly and clearly, it may be wise to take a brief and oversimplified look at how a human being makes sound. A man breathes in some air and then pushes it up through his larynx or voice box. Here the air vibrates the vocal chords, making sound which is amplified by the throat, parts of the head, and the upper part of the chest. The amplified sound is molded into recognizable patterns by the tongue, teeth, and lips. It is no trick at all to produce a blurred or unclear sound. All you need is to talk with your jaw clenched, or with no action on the part of your tongue and lips. The poker face has no place in good speech. There has to be action and vigor in the facial muscles, the mouth, and the tongue. If, for instance, you try to say "mama" without using your lips, no one can understand you. If you want to say "hit" but don't move your tongue smartly, it will be heard as "hid."

Here is a simple prescription to help you make sounds of sufficient force and clarity. Take in a good breath, relax your throat, and have action and movement in your mouth. Many men, especially those with an athletic background, tend to breath deeply. With them, the belt buckle, not the chest, rises and falls with each breath. This long column of air, controlled by the strong abdominal muscles, makes for strong, flexible sound production.

Enthusiasm, or even real interest, will bring variety of pitch to your voice without any conscious effort on your part. I have never heard a monotonous voice from a person who had feeling about his topic. A few people talk with such little breath that the voice is very light and inexpressive. The above prescription will help this speaker particularly.

One fault that beginning speakers often have is talking very, very fast. Perhaps it's an unconscious effort to make an unpleasant situation as short as possible, but in your first two or three talks, particularly in the first few sentences, watch out for it. Try to hold it down to your normal conversational rate. Of course, this will vary a great deal from one person to another. I understand, for instance, that the late President Franklin D. Roosevelt talked at a rate of about 115 words a minute, and Walter Winchell still produces about 220. It is often said that the public speaker must speak slowly enough to be understood, yet fast enough to hold attention. Extremes are certainly to be avoided. The occasional person with very rapid speech must be especially careful to speak very clearly and distinctly. Also his liberal use of the pause will help make for understanding.

YOUR LANGUAGE

Your words mark you. It is astonishing how much can be learned about a man's background, his ideas and ideals, and even his character, as you listen to him talk. Public speaking is revealing. One commonly used measure of a man is his ability to use the English language clearly and correctly. Often it is the difference that determines social acceptance or business promotion. On the other hand, in some areas nothing could matter less. Consequently, what effort, if any, the individual wants to make to improve his use of English is a personal decision. But to the ambitious man or to the man with pride, the accurate and correct use of language is as essential as being clean. While it takes quite a while for culture to appear in a man's speech, he can with determination learn to talk correctly in a rather short time. A good friend of mine was probably one of the most able infantry company commanders in World War II but he was rejected on account of his English by the board hearing applications for regular Army commissions. During the next few months this captain worked hard on correcting his mistakes, and when he returned to face the board again he was accepted.

Let's look at the really jolting mistakes. First of all, the double negative is something to get rid of. "I don't want no coke." "I don't need none." "Nobody does nothing about it." Another familiar usage is "ain't got no." An earnest effort to substitute any for no, anything for nothing, will correct this, but it won't be easy. You'll have to make a sustained fight, realizing that if you ever become surprised or frightened or suddenly angry, the old double negative can betray you again. Of course, ain't is never correct, nor is "he don't" in place of "he doesn't."

The past tense and the past participle of irregular verbs make trouble. "I seen it." "They done well." Once I heard a stirring speech end on the following sour note, "and the South had fell." There are only about twenty-five of these verbs that are often used. It should be no trick at all for any one with reasonable intelligence to learn these verbs and to use them properly.

Correct pronunciation is a necessary goal. There are regional differences, of course, and you will follow the best usage of your part of the country. I see no need to change the best speech of your area unless you are headed for a career where a particular accent would be awkward —the stage, movies, or TV, for instance. Any dictionary can give you acceptable pronunciations. Many Americans, though, do strange things with words. They have a tendency to add a sound. Athletic becomes *athaletic;* umbrella, *umburrella*. They also have a tendency to leave out a sound. Government becomes *govment;* help, *hep*. In addition they often substitute one sound for another. Extra becomes *extree*; experiment, *expeeriment*; stomach, *stomick*. Finally, they tend to reverse *er* and *re*. Hundred becomes *hunderd;* prepare, *perpare;* perspiration, *prespiration*. Watch out for errors of this type, and if you have any uncertainty check with the dictionary. Be careful about using a word from a foreign language unless you are sure and comfortable in its pronunciation. Nothing reveals a phony quicker than a mistake here.

Much has been written about the desirability of a large vocabulary. There is no doubt that it increases the scope of a man's understanding and of his ability to communicate. From the standpoint of money, as more than one study has shown, the higher a man's financial standing the greater his vocabulary is likely to be. From the speaker's standpoint, the appropriate, accurate, descriptive words can be most helpful in that they can create a mental picture for the members of the audience, a tremendous step toward holding attention and creating understanding. On the other hand vague, general language will either build no mental image at all or will make a different one in each mind present. Give considerable thought to vivid, accurate language in any talk you make, but don't make it a showcase for all your wares. The purpose of the speaker is to communicate, not to dazzle or to bewilder. What he says must be understood instantly because the audience cannot go back to listen to a puzzling sentence again. In reading, you can, of course. You can look up any word that is unclear, staying with a sentence or paragraph as long as you wish. But in speaking, there is no second chance. Therefore, the speaker must help the audience, no matter how well educated they are. For a speech, the shortest, simplest word that will convey the meaning is the best. If a word of one or two syllables will do the job as well as one of three or four syllables, the shorter word will be clearer and easier to understand every time. Use it.

Now let's look at the two main speaking situations and approach slowly and simply the problem of planning a talk.

CHAPTER 3

TWO SPEAKING SITUATIONS

Speaking to a group usually occurs under two somewhat different circumstances.

In one, a man who is a member of the group gets the attention of the chairman, rises in place, and "speaks from the floor."

In the other, the speaker is the invited guest of the group and usually addresses it from a lectern or a speaker's stand. Let's consider these two situations more fully.

TALKING FROM THE FLOOR

In almost every community in the nation there are clubs, groups, and organizations of every nature and description. The person, male or female, who is not part of one or more of these groups is difficult indeed to find. Consequently you, too, are most likely a member of some group. Sooner or later you will either be required to make a report or will wish to express an opinion or a feeling from the floor. You generally do this by stating a point, usually called the central idea or the subject sentence, and backing it up with supporting material to make the idea clear, interesting, or acceptable.

For instance, you might say, "Mr. Chairman, the finances of this club are in good condition. (Subject sentence) All dues are collected. All bills are paid. We have no indebtedness of any kind, and we have $340.00 in the bank, $140.00 more than at this time last year." (Supporting information and comparison) This is the simplest kind of talk, yet here we have the backbone of all talks—a statement plus support. Of course, the more support, the longer the talk.

Sometimes, the central idea or subject sentence quite naturally breaks up into two or three main points with support for each. For example, you could say, "Mr. Chairman, our social calendar is set for the rest of the quarter. (Subject sentence)

A. We have a good program for February. (Main point No. 1) Support consisting of information about the program—events, dates, places, etc.

B. We have a good program for March. (Main point No. 2) Support as above.

When you have two or more points, it helps the audience to follow you if you put a link or connection between the points. A word or phrase like *furthermore, in addition, another reason,* etc., at the end of what you have to say about one point will lead your listeners easily into the next point. Technically, this is called transition. It is a little thing for the speaker to do, but helpful both to the smoothness and to the clarity of his talk.

Now we come to a rather common situation—the subject sentence that quite naturally breaks into three main points, with support for each. For instance, you might say, "Mr. Chairman, we could have a successful dinner dance at Echo Lodge (subject sentence), because (link)

    A. It is accessible. (main point No. 1.
       (Support by use of in- Link: "in addition")
       formation, comparison)

    B. It is reasonably priced. (main point No. 2.
       (Support by use of in- Link: "and furthermore")
       formation, comparison)

    C. It has good facilities." (main point No. 3)
       (Support by use of information, comparison, testimony)

Three main points and support are, in my opinion, about as much as the average speaker should attempt. Some speech texts permit four, some as many as five, but I believe you will be well-advised to stay with no more than three for quite a while. You see, the amount and quality of support you have for each point is what makes that point clear, interesting, and acceptable. Then too, you want your audience to remember your subject sentence and your main points, so why make it hard for them? The average audience will find it much easier to keep your main points in mind if you limit them to three.

Notice that in each of the above little talks you had a clear purpose that was the base of the talk. In the first, your purpose was to make clear to the members the financial situation for the club; in the second, your purpose was to make clear to the members the social program for the rest of the quarter. In this kind of talk, where you are trying to make one thing clear, there is no particular reason for or against using the statement of your purpose as your subject sentence. But notice the difference in the third talk. Here your purpose is to convince the group that Echo Lodge is the best place for your dinner dance. A blunt statement of this purpose is likely to rub some members the wrong way. Many people bristle when they hear a speaker say, "I am going to do this or that to you." If you are trying to persuade people to believe or feel or do something, you will almost certainly get a better reception by converting your purpose into an audience-centered subject sentence. For instance, "You would all enjoy a dinner dance at Echo Lodge." We will come back to purpose later as the base on which all talks should be built.

TALKING FROM THE SPEAKER'S STAND

In this day and age, sooner or later, you will very likely find yourself at the speaker's table or behind the speaker's stand. It is a difficult situation to avoid, and there is no very good reason for trying to avoid it. Your talk can be almost as simply constructed as your talks from the floor. Your purpose, subject sentence, main points, and support are set up in the same way, but you will need two small additions, a little added to your beginning (an introduction) and a planned ending (a conclusion).

Why are any additions needed? Well, first, when you are talking from the floor as a member of a group, you usually find the other members ready and willing to listen. They know that your remarks will, or should, be guided by the interests and affairs of the group. This is usually a continuing situation where attention shifts from one speaker to another rather rapidly but seldom disappears entirely, because everything that is said concerns the group. When you confront a group from the speaker's stand, however, the situation can be different. Some people may still be eating. Others may be a little bored. In the brief time it takes you to reach the speaker's stand after you have been presented, the minds of some can easily wander. So it is imperative that you start your talk in some way that will result in attention. You will also be wise to give, early in the talk, a reason for the audience to listen. These two additions plus your subject sentence constitute the introduction of your talk. We go into this in detail just a little further along.

Second, when you are confronting an audience, you can't merely stop talking and sit down as you would if you were talking from the floor. If you leave the speaker's stand with no warning, it will startle an audience. They expect some indication of the end, a summing up or a special ending. Also from your standpoint as a speaker, this is your last chance to emphasize your points and you don't want to miss it. The expert speaker plans his ending with great care.

If you feel that an introduction and a conclusion will help in speaking from the floor, you obviously are not barred from using either or both, although usually they are unnecessary. But, when you are the speaker, they become vital, essential parts of your talk.

Now let's look at the plan for preparing a talk. With a little experience you can use as much or as little of this step-by-step plan as you need.

CHAPTER

4

BUILD THE TALK CAREFULLY

Preparing a talk, like any other construction project, must be guided by a clear plan if the work is to be done efficiently and effectively. Below is a simple series of steps which you should work out with care in building your talk. A rather detailed explanation of the first two steps follows, with a chapter later on each of the three main parts of a talk, steps 3 through 6.

STEPS IN SPEECH PREPARATION

First, a brief explanation to lead into step 1.

Your purpose is exactly what you are going to try to do in the talk—your goal, your target. Having this clearly in mind from the start is basic and vital to successful speech preparation and to a successful talk.

1. Determine a purpose suitable to:
   a. your audience
   b. your time limit
   c. the occasion
   d. yourself
2. Gather material
3. Plan the introduction
4. Plan the body
5. Plan the conclusion
6. Practice

STEP 1. Determining your purpose

You will agree, I am sure, that it is foolhardy to speak without a clear-cut, definite, distinct purpose. Yet, all too many public speakers do it. They talk *about* something and the talk will be as vague and disorganized to the minds of the audience as it obviously is in the mind of the speaker. Being clear about your exact purpose is the key to the preparation of a good talk. In class, I require each speaker to hand me a statement of his specific purpose at least a day ahead of time. Usually it is very clear, showing that the man wants his audience to understand this, or to enjoy that, to feel this, or to do that. Sometimes, though, I am given simply a title or a subject, "Highway Safety," or "Baseball," etc. This won't do. It is much too vague, too broad. The speaker must boil it down, clarify it in his own mind till he can say, "My purpose is to impress upon the members of 'X' fraternity three rules for highway safety," or, "My purpose is to have a group of Little Leaguers understand clearly how signals and signs are given in baseball." Now, from this solid base, the preparation of the speech can go ahead intelligently.

Your purpose and your audience

When you are speaking from the floor the relation of your purpose to the group is natural and easy because you will be talking directly to their interests, problems, and needs, which you know well. However, before you stand in front of a strange group, you must make a real effort to tie in your purpose with their interests, problems, and needs. A considerable portion of many speech texts is given to audience analysis. I agree that it would be helpful to a speaker to know the age group, the sex, the political affiliation, the educational background, the economic status, etc., of the audience in great detail. But few speakers have the staff or time for such research. The best I have been able to do through the years is to get some brief information from the man who is asking me to talk, items like "fifty professional men," "the graduating class, their parents and the student body of 'X' high school," "one hundred fifty members of 'Y' sorority." Even this amount of information is very, very helpful. It would be grossly unfair to say that if you know one professional man, or one sorority girl, you know them all, yet from a picture of one you can make a fairly good appraisal of the general area of interests and needs of the whole group. When you are invited to speak to a group, it will virtually always be on account of some particular interest, knowledge, skill, or authority which you possess. You will be talking in one of these areas and you will want to adjust your purpose to the reaction you believe possible from the audience which you will face. Most of your decisions here will rest on good common sense. But, don't forget to find out what you can about your audience. A man I know of thought he had been asked to speak at a special P.T.A. meeting because the head of that group had called him. When he appeared at the school auditorium to speak a week later, he was horrified to see it filled with about a thousand fifth, sixth, seventh and eighth graders. Then, much too late, he remembered he had not asked Mrs. A. who would be in his audience. The talk was not a success. Don't let this happen to you.

Your purpose and your time limit

Here you may gain or lose much good will. Practically all public speaking is arranged with a definite time limit. You are almost always invited to speak for fifteen minutes, thirty minutes, perhaps even an hour—but a definite time is specified. The luncheon, dinner, or meeting where you are to speak has planned a program, including your talk, that will end early enough for the people attending to reach their offices, duties, homes, in good time. A talk that exceeds the time limit noticeably will annoy the audience almost every time. For instance, some months ago, I attended a dinner after which an able young man was to talk for twenty minutes in a field interesting to all those present. At the end of nineteen minutes, everyone had a high opinion of the speaker, but as he continued through the forty-minute mark, just about all good will had disappeared. When he finally stopped at the end of an hour, amidst chair scraping and muttering, he was generally regarded as a dope of the first water. His mistake, of course, was in not relating his purpose to the time given him. Many speakers try to cover too much. Those who are beginning are often dismayed by the thought of speaking for say fifteen minutes and try to cover the whole field of their major interest in that time. Actually, by choosing a segment or a portion of that field which common sense says you can cover well in the allotted time and by adjusting your supporting material, you can be reasonably close to your time limit. No one is going to hold a stop watch on you. Your only danger lies in careless and discourteous disregard of your given time. It will help if you keep the length of your talk constantly in mind when choosing your purpose. By doing so, you can become surprisingly accurate. Of course, when talking on radio or TV, you have to be ready for very exact timing. The studio will help you by flashing time cards, but when the card says "Stop" and the red light goes out, you have either finished your talk or you are talking to yourself.

In courtesy to the other members of the group, any talk you make from the floor should be as brief as possible for you to accomplish your purpose clearly.

Your purpose and the occasion

This is largely a matter of common sense, as is so much of speech planning and speaking. You should not bring a complex or a controversial purpose to a group concerned with enjoyment and relaxation. Nor will you often bring a frivolous purpose to a serious occasion. Sometimes the occasion will give you a clue to your purpose. For instance, a speaker at a dinner commemorating the birth of General

Robert E. Lee will almost surely aim his purpose at some development of the character, philosophy, and achievements of Robert E. Lee.

Your purpose and you

Whatever your purpose, you must feel reasonably comfortable with it at worst, and enthusiastic about it at best. The more your heart is in your purpose, the easier the preparation of the talk, and the more effective the talk. If your purpose comes from your mind or your heart, you should have no trouble.

STEP 2. Gather Material

The man who speaks about something close to his mind or heart will quite often find enough material for a speech simply by thinking about his subject. As we have said before, most people are asked to speak because of some particular competence or experience and, as they think in those areas, they usually develop plenty of material for a talk. Naturally, the ideas, facts, examples, comparisons, etc., that come to mind should be jotted down to be arranged later. Of course, in some situations, the speaker feels the need to supplement his own experience with additional facts and other points of view. This usually presents no great problem, provided he starts early. From the United States government on down, almost all enterprises are glad to furnish information in reply to a written request. Often in a community there will be a man who is an authority or who is greatly experienced in a field. These people are actually pleased to be interviewed for speech material. And, of course, in every community there is a public library which will hold a host of material on almost any subject under the sun. Here it is part of the librarian's job to help you solve your problem. Just tell her what you need.

Now let's look at the talk itself.

CHAPTER 5

THE INTRODUCTION

Before we get started in this chapter may I ask you to look at a device which can become very useful to you once you become familiar with it. I call it a "Speech Preparation Guide" because it puts before you in outline form the essential make-up of the three main parts of the talk. Using this as a check-sheet, we'll show you how to build the introduction, body, and conclusion of your talk.

SPEECH PREPARATION GUIDE

Introduction

A. Get attention:
    pause
    humor
    curiosity
    special interest
    common ground

    significance of subject
    familiar reference
    honest compliment
    previous speaker said

B. Orient the audience: State very clearly your specific purpose or your central idea. If desirable, give background or preview.

C. Give the audience a reason for listening. (Rule of thumb: The Introduction takes about 10 per cent of total speech time.)

Body

The real speech—about 85 per cent of total time. The body consists of main points with supporting material for each, and a transition, or link, from one point to the next. Main points are natural divisions of your central idea. Supporting material makes them clear and acceptable to the audience. Consequently you must have few main points, three or less, in order to support each one adequately enough for the audience to understand, accept, and remember them.

A. Main point and supporting material

  (transition)

B. Main point and supporting material

Main points, like paragraphs in a theme or in a report, are arranged in some easy to follow sequence such as:

topic	space	cause-effect
time	problem-solution	importance

Supporting material is used to make a point clear, to make a point interesting, or to prove a point. Supporting materials and techniques which you will use consist of:

comparison or contrast	description
examples	restatement

evidence (facts or state-   illustration
ments of authorities)   information
explanation (who, what,   testimony
where, when, how)

To be sure that your support is clear and interesting (a big help in holding attention), check it for as many as possible of the following characteristics:

audience-centered   concrete   vivid
familiar   varied   amusing

Conclusion

A solid, short, clear ending—roughly 5 per cent of time. One or any combination of the following:

restate central idea   striking quotation
summarize main points   final appeal
brief story

Start early!

Now let's go back to the beginning of the guide, developing each item in detail. At the end of a good introduction, the speaker should have favorable attention and the audience should know clearly in what direction the speaker is headed and how the subject touches them. The introduction is a short part of the talk, and while the 10 per cent rule of thumb above is not to be considered exact, it does indicate clearly that no great amount of time should be taken in getting the talk started.

GETTING ATTENTION

It should be understood that any one of the devices for securing attention discussed below usually consists of only a sentence or two. Your job is to select the device you feel would best launch your particular talk. These follow without any particular order of preference.

Pause

As pointed out in the chapter on delivery, the pause can be an effective way of getting attention. If the speaker can keep quiet for just a few seconds before he starts his talk, that alone will be a big help in gaining the attention of the group.

Humor

A common American misconception is that every talk must start with a joke. There is nothing better, it is true, provided the joke is funny, is in good taste, and ties in with your purpose. However, if the joke is not funny and falls flat, the speaker may lose the interest of the audience from then on. Humor can be treacherous. When it works well, there is nothing better for the speaker; when it fails, there is nothing worse. It's a good idea to try out your joke a time or two on people similar to those who will be in the audience and be guided accordingly. Humor that is well accepted in the locker room will get a cold shoulder at P.T.A. meetings, and humor aimed at any particular group can annoy part of the audience. A funny story that has no connection with your topic does some good, but can leave you in an awkward spot. It is much better if there is some easy link between the story and your purpose or topic. No one loves humor more than I, but I am not at all sure that a person can be taught to use it well. I once heard Ed Wynn say that all jokes were variations of, I believe, seven basic situations. But even if these are taught, an individual in my opinion must have imagination, creativeness, and a real flair for humor to be able to handle it well consistently. It is wiser for some people not to try it in the public speaking situation. Be realistic about your chances of success as you consider trying it. Let's not forget, though, that the reward for success is high in good will and in attention.

Common ground

It is often helpful in getting favorable attention if the speaker can show that he has had the same experiences or background that most of the audience have had. For instance, the banker who reminds a group of farmers that he too was raised on a farm and is familiar with their problems by firsthand experience will establish common ground with them, and hence, will usually get favorable attention.

Significance of the subject

A statement to the audience of the importance of your topic is a good way to start. It gets attention and gives the audience a reason to listen, but the rest of the talk must make good the promise. If you say, "I am going to talk to you parents about something that is vital to the health of your children," it had better be or you are in trouble.

Familiar reference

It is surprising that simply mentioning a familiar name, place, or thing can create attention and interest, but it certainly does. I think we can all remember times in our daily lives when we have overheard some familiar reference and have been tempted to get closer to hear more.

"As I drove out Sunset Boulevard past the N.B.C. Studio," will get the attention of one audience. A reference to Mickey Mantle or Willie Mays would be better for another. You use terms familiar to the particular audience even though you may or may not be equally familiar with them. For instance, I have heard three men from distant places talk here, yet each one started by referring to two or three things familiar to us around the campus.

Special interest

If you know that your audience is almost all from one group (students, farmers, union members, etc.) you can get attention by mentioning whatever is of special interest to the group. With the above groups, it could be grades, price supports, or a shorter work week. To be effective, this device can be used only when your audience is a solid group and you know what its strong interests are.

An honest compliment

This can be good if the compliment is justified and the speaker is sincere about it. You can usually find something to say that is both honest and pleasant about any audience, but be careful of overdoing it. Then of course, occasionally you will face a group that has really done something that merits praise, which makes the compliment both easy and sincere. It is a good way to start, but don't let it get too lush or thick.

The previous speaker said . . .

Once in a while someone talking ahead of you will provide such a fine lead-in to your talk that you abandon what you had planned and use this instead. You become alert for such an opportunity as you grow more experienced, but obviously you can't count on it and should always have your own plan for starting your talk.

ORIENTING THE AUDIENCE

When you finished the very first step in speech preparation, determining your exact purpose, you just about took care of this important part of your introduction. Now all you need do is to state the purpose clearly. If you prefer to phrase it as a subject sentence, state that clearly. The audience should be completely sure where your talk is headed. If they don't understand it now, you have very probably lost them for the whole talk. Occasionally a speaker will want to tell how he became interested in a particular topic or will want to give a little general background. This is perfectly appropriate. Also, a speaker sometimes wants to tell briefly how he is going to develop the talk. One way, called an "initial summary," is to state his reasons or his main points at this time in the order in which he expects to talk about them. This shows the audience where he is going and tends to make his talk easier to follow.

GIVE A REASON FOR LISTENING

You may give the audience a reason for listening either before or after you make your purpose clear. The important thing is that somewhere in the introduction you show the audience that they will benefit in some way, little or big, by listening to your talk. As soon as they hear a subject sentence, many people think, "How in the world does that touch me?" If you can answer their question, you have a hold on their attention through the whole talk. Let me give you an example or two. "I hope to increase your understanding and liking of baseball by explaining how signals are given on the field." "The answer to any etiquette problem you can think of is in the book I am going to talk about tonight." "We all want to save money, etc." There should be no problem about a tie-in with the audience. If you can think of no way that your purpose would benefit or affect the audience, you don't want to use it. Get another purpose that does.

Now let's go on to the main part of the talk, the body.

CHAPTER 6

THE BODY

Here is your real talk, the place where you attempt to accomplish your purpose in speaking. As you remember, it was pointed out earlier that the body may consist simply of support for the one idea you are trying to put across, but that often an idea may logically and usefully be divided into two or three parts. In the latter case, the main ideas and support for them form the body of your talk. Occasionally a subject sentence can be broken down into five or six main thoughts, but I strongly advise that you select only the two or three which will best serve your purpose and build your talk around them. You are trying to get the audience to understand, accept, and remember your thoughts, for which you need plenty of support. If you have too many points you will find them difficult to support adequately in a limited time, and the audience will not be able to remember them no matter how long your talk is.

THE BODY 45

These main points are really topics which may be arranged in a variety of ways—often called "patterns" or "sequences"—which help the audience to understand and remember them. For instance:

A. The Ford in 1920,
B. The Ford in 1940,
C. The Ford in 1961,

is a chronological or time arrangement pattern.

A. The state college in the East,
B. The state college in the South,
C. The state college in the West,

is an arrangement by geographic location, sometimes called a "space arrangement."

A. Professors are underpaid.
B. Real estate taxes should be raised.

This arrangement is a problem–solution arrangement.

A. People are careless in the woods.
B. The loss from forest fires is tremendous.

This is a cause–effect setup. Sometimes the reverse, effect–cause, can be used well.

A. Most important point	A. Next most important point
B. Least important point	B. Least important point
C. Next most important point	C. Most important point

Here the arrangement is obviously by importance. Notice the difference. A mighty argument still goes on as to which is more effective. Take your choice, but be sure you start and finish with your stronger points, leaving the weak in the middle, which is where the weak end up anyway.

Now let's assume that you have selected two main points and have arranged them suitably. In order to make each point clear and interesting and perhaps to prove it, you must support the point adequately. As you become more experienced, you will become more comfortable in using the various supporting materials listed on page 37. There are as many different lists of supporting materials as there are fleas on a hound dog, and this one is about as good as any. With experience, you will learn to choose the supporting materials which best develop each point. For instance, let's say that one main point of your talk, or the only point of your talk is "Ted Williams is a great hitter." You might support this with information, facts and figures about his record. You could give the example of his hitting a home run with the bases full in such and such a game. You could compare his record with that of other fine hitters. You could describe the last-second flick of the wrists and the smooth swing with which he hits the ball. You could give testimony about his hitting from such well-known authorities on baseball as Casey Stengel and Dizzy Dean. Finally, as you leave the point, you might restate what a fine hitter he is. You have used, then, six different kinds of supporting material to develop your point. You can probably see how you could talk for ten minutes or three minutes, depending on the choice and amount of support.

Perhaps a little information about supporting material would be in order. Let's run down the list, made up with no special order of preference.

1. *Comparison or contrast*

This is a very good way to help the audience understand. A comparison or contrast with something people know well helps them get a clear mental picture of what you are talking about. For instance, "She looks like Marilyn Monroe."

Comparison is particularly useful in giving an idea of size. Dimensions in feet or yards mean something different to every listener, but if you say that a submarine is just about as long as a football field, or that the Pyramids are about ten times as high as a familiar building, every listener gets a mental picture that is clear and similar to his neighbor's.

Comparison in the form of suggestion is a good technique in persuasion. The idea is that if another group much the same as ours has done such and such a thing, why can't we, too? Children seem to know this almost instinctively. I've probably heard a hundred children say, "Mom, Johnny Jones is in my grade and he lives right down the street and his daddy is a prof too, and he can go to the movies tonight, so why can't I?" The defense rests.

2. *Evidence or statements of authority*

A basic element of proof and of belief. You can't expect people to accept your word for some things and you have to prove any assertion by using facts, examples, testimony. Of course a statement by an authority is acceptable evidence only in the field of his competency. For instance, my statement that Brown is a more effective speaker than Johnson could be used as evidence, but my statement that Bowl of Roses is a better racehorse than Carry Back is worthless as evidence because I have no standing whatsoever in the world of horse racing. Watch out for unsupported assertions in your talk and in any talk you hear. It remains a mere opinion unless there is evidence to back it up.

3. *Examples*

Here is a splendid and versatile kind of support. It can be used to help understanding, to create interest, and, when three or four are strung together, can be effective proof. More than two thousand years ago Aristotle said there should be at least one example for every point in a talk. I'll put myself in good company by agreeing. An example is actually a specific instance, a small story with facts, names, dates, and places. It can make a vague statement become mighty clear. For instance, if you say, "Wine can be intoxicating," everyone in the audience will have a different picture of what you mean. But if you go on and say, "For example, early Saturday evening Tom Grady drank a fifth of cheap wine and was found at nine o'clock that night flat on his back in the gutter at the corner of Magnolia and College Streets with his arms folded on his chest, his eyes shut, completely unconscious of this world," then all the group gets a clear picture of what you mean. In my opinion, it is almost impossible for the beginning speaker to use too many examples. They are a tremendous help to the audience, and in turn, to the speaker.

4. *Explanation*

This is the familiar who, what, where, when, how that spell out information for the group. When handled correctly, explanation makes for clarity and interest. In using it the speaker must determine whether he is seeking general, broad understanding or specific, detailed working knowledge. For instance, the explanation given to visitors of the workings of a recoilless weapon would stress the broad, general differences between this and a conventional gun; but the explanation given to the soldiers who are going to use it would be much more detailed and complete. Also in any "how to" explanation make sure you start with the very first step and keep each step in proper sequence as you go. Don't tell them to push the starter before you tell then to turn the ignition key.

5. *Description*

The word-picture can be useful for clarity, interest, and belief. The ability to use vivid, colorful, accurate language is not a gift that everyone has, but we can all try. Some of us have the very bad habit of using the same word to describe everything. A baby is cute, an elephant is cute, an Atlas rocket is cute, etc. We can do better than that. We are all capable of concrete, specific language which, of course, is a big help to the audience's understanding of the talk. Which of the following sentences gives you the more vivid impression? a) The boy was fat, or b) The little boy was so fat that he seemed to have huge red apples stuffed in his cheeks and his eyes looked like raisins pressed deep into pink dough.

6. *Illustration*

In the speech sense, this word is not a drawing or an illustration such as you see in a book or magazine. It means a long story, a narrative, an extended example. Often when a speaker's purpose is simply to have the audience enjoy his speech, he will have just one point and support it entirely by a long story or narrative. For instance, his point might be "Mardi Gras is fun" and his only support the story of how he spent Shrove Tuesday in New Orleans. If the story is kept moving and is not allowed to drag, it can hold attention and interest, as many of us learned in childhood.

7. *Information*

As we all realize, this is the tremendous area of news, knowledge, statements, names, places, events, etc. The bulk of most speeches is information no matter what the purpose of the speaker. An audience must be given knowledge before it can understand and it can only have interest if it has some understanding. Whether you are trying to make something clear to a group or trying to interest them or trying to get them to do something, information will be the basic part of your support. You owe it to your audience and to yourself to get your information from a reliable source and to use only what is accurate and clear.

8. *Restatement*

As we have commented elsewhere, the audience must understand instantly what the speaker says or it will fall behind and get lost. Restatement is a way of helping those who fell behind and of emphasizing your point to those who heard it the first time. It is a good idea to rephrase your purpose or subject sentence and to restate it two or three times during your talk, and it is an equally good idea to rephrase and to restate each main point before you go on to the next. This is a big help toward clarity and emphasis. We are all familiar with restatement as an advertising technique. It works there and it works in a speech.

9. *Testimony*

In speech, testimony, in the best sense, is the use by the speaker of a quotation from an authority well and favorably known to the audience. The speaker says, in effect, "You may not think my opinion on this subject amounts to very much, but, look, this authority you know is saying the same thing." This beyond doubt strengthens the speaker's position and is therefore used often. If you want to quote from an authority unknown to your audience, it is wise to identify him first. Testimony also includes the word of the man who has been or done or used something. With one exception, it is usually not too valuable in a speech unless the person is well known. The exception is the speaker's own personal experience in the area in which he is talking, which contributes to his authority before the group.

Once you have chosen your main points and the support to go with them, it is good to take one last look to see if there is anything more you can do to hold attention, a basic problem in every speech.

Way back when you were selecting your purpose, you considered its suitability for this particular audience. This audience-centered point of view should hold all through the talk. If an audience can see how a subject touches them, that it holds meaning for them, and that it is in frames of reference they understand, this approach alone will be a big help in holding attention.

As we have already seen that the familiar tends to be interesting, may I suggest that you check your comparisons and examples to make sure they will be familiar to your audience. For instance, the example of an automobile accident in Oregon will not interest an Auburn, Alabama, audience as much as a very similar accident on the Montgomery Highway and vice versa.

Concreteness—the use of specific, clear, accurate language—helps build a mental picture and is a real factor in holding interest. Beware of vague, general terms. No mental picture goes with them, and, all too soon, attention is lost.

I think you'll agree that there should be a change of pace in your supporting material. Different kinds of support, variety, make for interest.

Vivid descriptive language helps hold attention but is difficult to fit into all kinds of support and all kinds of situations. Use it as much as you can. Statistics can be reduced in proportion and used occasionally to startle a group. For instance, "The figures just published by the National Highway Safety Board show that by the end of this year five of you people sitting before me will be lying dead or injured on some highway."

The amusing, the humorous, the funny, the witty can do wonders for a talk. If you can work any of these in and do it effectively, go to it. There's nothing better for attention and interest.

Now let's talk for a minute about something that isn't supporting material but still can be most helpful to a

THE BODY

speaker—the visual aid. A visual aid is something the audience can see which helps their understanding. A speaker is sometimes his own visual aid—for instance, the coach showing the boys how to hold and throw a curve ball. But usually the visual aid is a blackboard, graph, chart, picture, model, or piece of equipment the speaker uses to help make his meaning more clear. The audience benefits by better understanding, but the speaker benefits, too, by having something to do or to work with, which almost always reduces his tension considerably. If you are going to use a visual aid of some sort, it has to be big enough for the audience to see. This would seem to be obvious, indeed, yet many speakers don't adhere to it, losing much of the usefulness of the aid. Then, of course, the speaker has to get himself out of the way so the group can see. Here, too, you often find that speakers can be thoughtless. In addition, the speaker must always remember that the main focus of his attention must be on the group. It is a strong temptation to look at and talk to the board or graph or object. Try to keep it to the barest minimum, looking at and talking to the audience as much as you possibly can. Some talks lend themselves to visual aids; others do not. Use visual aids at every opportunity. You and the audience will both gain.

Now let's put the finishing touches on your job of speech preparation.

CHAPTER

7

THE FINISHING TOUCHES

All that remains now in your speech preparation is to plan an ending and to practice your talk.

The conclusion is a short, solid, important part of the talk. It is your last chance to reach the audience and it is a notice to them that the talk is ending. Of the different types of conclusions, I would judge that the combination of summarizing the main points and restating the central idea is used most often, but from time to time there will be a quotation or story which focuses the central thought of a talk so well that it can make an impressive ending. In talks where a speaker is trying to make something clear, he will often include in the conclusion a statement telling the audience where they can find more information on the subject. The talk to persuade almost always ends with a final appeal, such as, "Let's all go to the polls tomorrow and vote for our next Congressman, Mr. Dennis Pogo."

THE FINISHING TOUCHES 55

Watch out for one thing that often happens to beginning speakers. You'll almost certainly leave something out of your talk, and quite often you will think of it just as you are ending. It is a temptation to haul it in then and there. Don't do it. It will just throw the audience off and mess up your planned ending. Then, too, a speaker will occasionally end his talk by saying, "I thank you." This puzzles me unless the man feels he has made a sorry talk and is grateful to the group for being considerate. If the talk is clear and interesting, as it should be, the audience should logically thank the speaker. At any rate, the conclusion merits careful planning. It should be short, a hard blow, leaving the audience in no doubt about what you were driving at and that you are now through. This is your last impression on the audience. Try to make it a good one.

Now comes a job that must be done: practicing the talk. It is generally agreed that the best way to practice is on your feet and out loud, but a few people, and I'm one of them, find this difficult to do and prefer to run through the talk silently. It helps to make a skeleton outline with only your subject sentence, main ideas, an indication of what support you are using for each point, and how you are going to start and stop the talk. Go all the way through your talk once without looking at the card. You'll leave out something, of course, but you'll be surprised at how many of the thoughts stay in your mind if you have made a real effort to plan the talk. And these are what you want to remember, not a string of words. The words will change quite a bit every time you go through the talk. Notice that you have written no manuscript, nor do you need to. The last thing you want to do is try to memorize a series of written words. You can pretty easily remember the ideas in a well-planned talk. Just talk to these ideas. Professionally, this is called the extemporaneous speech. It has many advantages over the memorized speech as pointed out in the section which follows shortly.

After you have gone through your talk once and have refreshed your memory by looking at your outline or line-up, go through it again. Each time you will leave out less. There is no rule for the exact number of times to practice. People differ and talks differ in difficulty, but you should practice until you feel you are in command of your talk. Don't try to do it all at one sitting. Two practice sessions a day for three days will almost always give better results than six sessions in one day. This is one good reason for starting your preparation early.

Every speaker must decide whether or not to use notes. There's nothing wrong with using them provided they are on cards which are easy to handle and are written big enough for the speaker to see without bending down to them. The main danger of notes is that they can become a barrier to direct communication if the speaker refers to them a great deal, especially if he has to duck down to do it. The beginning speaker is usually comforted by the thought of having some notes with him. The skeleton outline mentioned before should be enough unless the speaker has many figures to use or a long quotation to read. Incidentally, it is not necessary to say "quote" and "unquote" before and after a quotation. Just pick up the card, read it, and put it down. That and the natural change of voice will bracket the quote for the audience.

THE FINISHING TOUCHES

May I encourage you, though, to speak without notes? First of all, audiences like it. They feel the speaker has paid them the compliment of getting good and ready, and that he really knows what he is talking about. Second, the speaker is not tied to the lectern. He is free to move as he wants and where he wants. This makes for good, direct, conversational delivery. Third, it is much easier to do than most people realize. Usually you are asked to speak, as we have said before, in some area where you are especially competent. You know this field well. Consequently, all you need to remember is a sequence of two or three main thoughts that you want to present. You need no cards for that. For instance, a golf pro could talk for a long time without notes on "How to Putt" simply by lining up a natural sequence of ideas, "The Grip," "The Stance," "The Put." I urge every beginner to prepare thoroughly but also to be determined not to use notes. Have the spunk to start that way and stay with it. The rewards are worthwhile.

Now let's look at the problems of the memorized talk and of a talk which is read.

Many Americans assume incorrectly that a speech must be committed to memory. The idea is kept alive by several nationally sponsored oratorical contests for high school students, but beyond that area the memorized speech has virtually disappeared from the American scene. There are several good reasons for this.

First of all, it takes a tremendous amount of time to write out a speech in manuscript form and commit it to memory. Few people in this busy age can spare the time.

It also seems inefficient to me because talking from a skeleton outline (the extemporaneous speech) is a much simpler, easier, more effective method to accomplish the same purpose.

The second reason the memorized speech is falling out of favor is that the very real danger of forgetting is always present. In memorized speeches, you are linking a multitude of symbols together in your mind. If anything happens to break the linkage, you are virtually helpless. There is not much to do except wait and pray that something will jog your memory and enable you to continue. You are likely to forget because material learned in the peace and quiet of your study often seems to be very well learned but turns out to be learned too poorly to stand the pressure of the speaking situation. I remember an oratorical contest in which one youngster was going a mile a minute until suddenly no sound came from his open mouth. He stood speechless in front of the group for one minute by my watch—which may not seem long to you, but try it some time. Perspiration was popping out all over the boy's face when, just as suddenly as he had stopped, the flow of words started again and he finished in triumph. There is not much sense in taking on the added worry and pressure that the memorized speech brings to the speaking situation.

The third problem is that it takes a very clever person to make the memorized talk sound conversational. All too often, the speaker sounds like a grammar school student reciting something by rote. There is likely to be little real awareness of communicating with the audience. The speaker's thoughts so often appear to be turned in on himself, as of course they will be in trying to keep the flow of symbols coming on smoothly. There is a feeling on the part of the audience that the speaker is looking at them but not really seeing them. Moreover, the memorized talk permits no flexibility because the speaker cannot adjust it to meet any evident confusion on the part of the audience. In fact, he will in all probability be unaware of any audience reaction, good or bad. It is true that occasionally a man has the skill to make memorized material sound conversational but such a person is rare. I feel that it is not worth the trouble and effort to find out whether or not you have this skill. Chances are that you don't.

The last problem with the memorized talk is that it is very difficult to produce a manuscript in which the written language closely resembles spoken language. In writing, we tend to use more complicated structure than in speaking, more formal language, and often longer words. Even though the delivery of a memorized speech is good, quite often the construction of the language reveals that the speech is actually memorized. There is nothing so bad about this if the construction of the language does not interfere with communication. You realize, of course, that the speaker's words must be instantly intelligible to the group, while a paragraph in a book may be studied as long as the person wants, or as long as he must to understand it.

I hope that after these strong warnings of danger and trouble you will feel no need to attempt to make a memorized speech.

While we are talking about problems, we might as well take a quick look at another pitfall, the speech that is read. Let's leave that to the executive who is so busy that someone else must write his speech for him, or to the person who is so important that any inaccuracy in his speech could cause misunderstanding and real trouble. The highly placed executive may have somebody on his staff construct a speech as directed along certain lines and perhaps have a chance to look it over only once or twice before he reads it. For the average man, though, writing out a manuscript and reading the speech require a lot of time and considerable skill. The simple mechanics of oral reading regrettably are not always as simple as they seem. The temptation is to center all attention on the manuscript rather than on the audience, which often makes for an expressionless, difficult-to-understand communication. If, by any chance, you find yourself in a position where you feel you must read a speech, be sure to practice it ahead of time. The more often you can break contact with the manuscript, the better. The idea is to become so familiar with the construction and meaning of the manuscript that you can pick up a sentence or perhaps a short paragraph at a glance. This takes much of the curse off reading and makes for a clearer talk and a more expressive delivery.

CHAPTER 8

"BY SWEETNESS"

A literal translation of persuasion is "by sweetness." A definition of persuasion is "the attempt to influence people's attitudes toward something"—by words, of course, so far as this book is concerned. Yet many of us do not understand the relationship between these two ideas as we use persuasion in our daily lives. We back a man into a corner with an argument and force him into grudging agreement. We say, "Let's go to the movies because *I* want to." We try to command our equals. The results are often far from the best and resentment usually accompanies them. To change is difficult, though, because for most of us it would require a basic change in outlook, to make us think of the other person and not just of our own satisfaction. If we would let the man we are crushing with argument have an escape hatch so he could agree but save face, if we would say, "Let's go to the movies because *you'd* enjoy them," if we would request, not command, life would be smoother, we'd all be happier, and we'd get a lot more done.

While this change would be pleasant in our private lives, it is absolutely imperative for a public speaker. If he is to be effective at all, he simply must talk from the standpoint of his audience. He must use the "we" or "you" approach, and he must show the audience that what he advocates will benefit them in some way, little or big. They must see that what the speaker proposes relates to them and their welfare. You remember that during the introduction of a talk, the audience is likely to be thinking, "What's this to me?" That question must be answered, particularly in a talk where the whole purpose is persuasion. Actually, if there is sincerity in persuasion as there certainly should be, the "you" or "we" approach is natural and easy. Or to turn it around, if what the speaker proposes will not help the audience in some way, how can he have the gall to attempt it? None of this means that the speaker is forbidden to use the word "I." Of course, he isn't. He may use it in testimony, in example, in explanation, in recounting an experience, in any way that will make his position stronger and clearer. And often, the fact that there is a personal relationship between a speaker and the position he is taking in his speech, is interesting to the audience and effective. To repeat, however, his approach should always be from the "you" or "we" standpoint.

To be successful in persuasion, the speaker must attain four goals.

First, he must hold attention. It is obvious that a talk

cannot influence people to think, feel, believe, or do anything unless they hear it. The speaker must make a special effort. The "you" approach, concrete language, and the other attention-getting devices can be a big help, along with thorough preparation and enthusiastic, sincere delivery.

Second, he must be clear. Here too, obviously, a group cannot be persuaded unless it understands exactly what the speaker's position is, how it touches them, and what they are supposed to do about it. Again, straightforward, concrete language, support that is clear and in familiar frames of reference for the group, and simple, clear organization, all make for understanding. Main points or reasons, especially, should be clearly stated and restated. The link or transition from one point to another helps the group follow the speaker's train of thought. His conclusion should plainly reinforce his position.

Third, he must secure belief. This can be quite an enterprise, but often belief alone will result in successful persuasion. Of course, the audience can't get far enough along to believe the speaker unless they are interested in what he is talking about and understand it, so those first two goals are even more vital. Naturally, much of belief is built on evidence, facts, examples, testimony. This seems self-evident, yet many speakers fall into the trap of the bare assertion or the unsupported opinion. In addition to supplying evidence, the speaker can also make good use of suggestion, as was pointed out earlier. Often an appeal to the emotions can be most persuasive. Man likes to think he is a creature of reason, but his emotions lie close to the surface. A harrowing description of a starving child will stir our sympathy and bring us to action more rapidly, in all probability, than will the citing of statistical evidence of widespread starvation. And so it is with an appeal to other emotions. It goes without saying that a force as powerful as emotion should be used only with kindness, decency, and honesty.

Fourth, he must show that his proposal answers some want or need of the group. As we all know, human beings have a multitude of wants and needs. These are sometimes very broadly classified in two groups: physiological and social. Often a speaker will attempt to fill a need or want that requires no particular action on the part of the group. What he seeks for the group is, perhaps, enjoyment, education, appreciation, inspiration. Often, though, he will seek action. For instance, "Let's all contribute blood to the Red Cross." Occasionally, there will be a real or imagined obstacle to group action which the speaker must overcome by offering a plan or a solution, if his talk is to be successful. It should go without saying that it is unwise and improper for the speaker to ask the group to do anything it does not have the power or skill or right to do.

Persuasion is a field of great depth and breadth. We have barely touched upon it here, yet the speaker who can achieve the four goals above will almost certainly be successful in a wide range of honest, sincere persuasion. For those who want to go into it further, any good library has books on psychology, group behavior, selling, and persuasion. Just tell the librarian your problem.

With even the most guarded approach to persuasion should go a warning. The art or skill of persuasion is not controlled entirely by the good, decent, honorable men of this world. The deceitful and the unscrupulous can and do use it. Your best defense as a listener is to realize that the propagandist wants you to act without reflection, that he wants you to feel or to believe or to do something without thinking about it seriously. Obviously then, your protection lies in studying the situation, evaluating, and comparing before you commit yourself. We all need to listen more intently and intelligently when things important to us are being discussed. Of course, we listen for different reasons: to learn, to be polite, to enjoy, etc. But to things aimed at our minds and hearts, and pocketbooks for that matter, we can and should listen better than many of us do. May I suggest a pattern that can be helpful?

First of all, make a conscious effort to listen. Pay strict attention, the kind of attention a student pays to a review lecture directly before a test. A strong will can help. Of course, in the public speaking situation, the able speaker will help the audience to pay involuntary, or effortless, attention by using the various devices at his disposal.

Second, keep an open mind. Don't be prejudiced by the fact that one speaker has a mustache, or that another one looks dowdy. Hear them out. If an idea comes along that is new, different or even distasteful to you, don't tune out the speaker. And most emphatically of all, if you don't agree with the speaker, resist the temptation to form a rebuttal starting at that very moment. Hear him through. Perhaps by the end there will be no need for a rebuttal.

Finally, weigh, analyze, and evaluate what you hear. Is the speaker offering any evidence, facts, testimony? Is he using unsupported assertions? In the light of your experience and of your common sense, is the man talking sense or nonsense? What is his motive? Is he sincere? How much has he done to develop belief? Is what he suggests just and legal?

This kind of attitude on the part of the individual or group listener can make life more difficult for the propagandist, the purveyor of deceit, the confidence man, the advocate of the hard sell, but the honest, decent speaker will welcome it. The speaker who, as the Psalm says, "doeth the thing which is right and speaketh the truth from his heart" has nothing to fear from a critical audience.

CHAPTER 9

MAY I PRESENT?

Almost everyone in the United States is a member of an organization or a club. You are undoubtedly one of these people. As such, you will almost certainly face the situation sooner or later of introducing a speaker, presenting an award, or even receiving an award. These little talks are no problem if their purpose is understood and if they are kept simple.

Let's look first at the business of introducing a speaker. Your purpose is to place the speaker in a favorable light. To do this you must obviously know the speaker's name exactly and precisely, his position or title, and something of his history and achievements. Quite often the speaker will tell you, if you ask him, just about what he would like to have you touch upon in your introduction. Often the speaker will be a member of your own group or community so well-known to the audience that, to use the trite phrase, he needs no introduction. Then two or three sentences showing good will are all you need, the general idea being that you like the man and are glad he can be with the group.

However, when the speaker is not so intimately known to the audience, it is your duty to tell them some of his accomplishments. Be careful not to let this grow into a life history and fervent eulogy. Remember you are not the star of this show. Your job is just to set up the speaker favorably and pleasantly. Usually the listing of a few of the highlights of the speaker's career plus some courteous comment is enough. Don't overdo it. Don't take too long—and have his name and title straight.

As you may have noticed by this time I am strongly in favor of clarity, simplicity, and courtesy in speech. All three apply when you present an award. Usually a simple, clear statement of what the man has done to merit the award, the name of the donor, a very brief history of the award (if a history is appropriate), and a sentence about your pleasure in presenting it will fill the bill well. Whenever the speaker has the poor taste (in my opinion) to turn loose an endless blast of exaggerated praise, I always feel sorry for the recipient. He is entitled to his moment of glory, of course, but if it lasts much more than a moment in this captive situation, he and a lot of others in the audience start squirming. So let's keep this talk, like the introduction, clear, accurate, pleasant, and short.

Many people, I believe, go astray in what they say in accepting an award. There is a tendency to try to thank everyone who had the faintest relationship with the accomplishment from the day of the man's birth on. This to me is both unwise and unnecessary, resulting usually in a dreary list which often becomes ridiculous, as in the case of the All-American football player who ended up thanking his dog. Another trap that many fall into in this situation is an unaccustomed and overwhelming humbleness. They just can't understand what they did to deserve all this. They can't believe that a mistake hasn't been made because nothing they have ever done entitles them to such recognition. This does not sit well with me, especially when I know, as I have in some cases, that the man's words in public are a far cry from what he has said in private. Here, too, let's keep the thing simple and courteous. I believe something as simple as "Thank you very much, Mr. Jones. I appreciate the honor of this award," is perfectly adequate.

These little talks are sometimes known as "courtesy talks." Let's handle them that way. Just be pleasant, accurate, brief.

CHAPTER 10

LEARN TOGETHER

Learning together to make an effective talk is perfectly feasible. All you need is a room, a plan and some helpful comments. The beginner can make these comments almost as well as the professional, especially if he has read the text. It is easy for anyone to tell when the speaker does not look at the group, when he can't be heard, when he has a distracting mannerism, when the talk has no introduction or no conclusion, when the meaning is not clear, etc. The important thing is for the beginner to have several speaking experiences. Usually in an adult group assembled voluntarily there is strong motivation to learn and to do well, which is a splendid starting point for the beginner. There is nothing about giving a good little talk which will not yield to some determination and to some work. You will be surprised at the progress a group can make by going through one course together.

Let's look at one suggested arrangement of talks in such a course, and then at the simple mechanics of each meeting. The mechanics will vary according to the circumstances of the course, and a teacher can, if needed, substitute or add further assignments.

THE COURSE

Talk no. 1. Your purpose is to tell the group some facts about yourself—where you were born, where you went to school, where you work, where you live, what you like to do, marital status, etc. Each member introduces himself in this way to the group. Let's start with a brief talk, two to three minutes. Afterwards let the group comment as it wishes about any facts in any talk, but there should be no criticism of the delivery or the talk itself.

Talk no. 2. Your purpose is to have the audience enjoy some experience you have had or some incident you know about. This usually can go in one of two directions, to amuse or to interest. For instance, an account of your youthful experience in Farmer Bell's melon patch could be mildly amusing to the group; your account of your visit to Carlsbad Caverns, quite interesting. This talk is often made up of one point supported by an illustration, a story—about five minutes. A few constructive comments this time.

Talk no. 3. Your purpose is to make clear to the audience how something is made, or how something is used, or how something is done, or how something happened, or what something means, and you are to help make your meaning clear by using a visual aid. For instance, your purpose is to make clear to the group the traditional meaning of the main lines in one's hand, which you do with the help of a diagram on paper or on a blackboard. About five or six minutes. Avoid tackling too big a process here, such as trying to explain and demonstrate each step a peach takes from the tree through the canning factory to your kitchen table. By this time the talk should be complete technically, and constructive comments on the talk as well as on the delivery are in order.

Talk no. 4. Your purpose is to try to influence the attitude of the audience toward something. Try to take a position that is backed by your mind and your heart, and talk, of course, from the standpoint of the audience. Notice that the last talk in the course is also persuasion. It might save a little trouble to pick out a central idea for this talk and one for the last talk at the same sitting. Both about six minutes. Comments, of course. Permit the speaker to defend his position, if the need develops, but don't let any discussion last so long that it causes the elimination of a following talk.

Talk no. 5. Your purpose is to introduce one member of the group to the rest of the group in a favorable light. The simplest way to do this is to pair off for preparation and then have one of the pair introduce the other and vice versa. You can play this straight or let your imagination go and pretend you are introducing anyone you wish to the group. Keep it brief, two to three minutes at the longest.

Talk no. 6. Your purpose is to present pleasantly an award, a gift, a scholarship, a certificate of merit, etc., to a member of the group, whose purpose, in turn, is to accept it gracefully. Here, too, it is easy to pair off in preparation and to reverse the talks later. Just dream up any honor or award you wish. It's the experience of doing both these little jobs that counts.

Talk no. 7. Your purpose is to try the second or third talk again, with a different central idea, of course. Choose whichever talk you prefer or whichever you feel would benefit you most. This talk should show improvement in delivery and in organization.

Talk no. 8. Your purpose is to repeat the fourth assignment, naturally with a different central idea.

The impromptu talk

This is the talk given on the spur of the moment with no special preparation. This is a most useful tool in a beginning course to give the speaker easy, added appearances in front of the group. It usually takes the form of one point plus support. There are several ways to set up this situation.

If the chairman is ingenious enough, he

can ask each member a simple question. For instance, "Joe, what do you think of the New York Yankees?" or "Helen, what about the rumor that the very pointed toe is soon to be out of style?"

Another way is to have each member of the group turn in a list of five or six simple topics to the chairman who will then make a master list, eliminating any duplication, and numbering each topic. Then he can ask a member to pick any number from, say, one to forty. The member picks number 17, which is "The Alamo," and up he comes.

For further variety, the chairman can ask a member to speak about a pleasant experience, a painful experience, his favorite book, meal, movie star, etc.

Toward the end of the course, you can use a little plan that usually goes over well. Ask a member to say out loud the first noun that enters his mind. Then call on another member to talk about it. And, of course, repeat this process until everyone has been before the group.

You are interested in having a man talk to the audience, not in literal factual answers. Therefore, it is perfectly permissible for a speaker to evade one topic and take off in another direction. For instance, he might say, "I'm afraid I don't know much about the Philharmonic, but Al Hirt and his Dixieland combo are by far the best in that field," etc.

Every member of a beginning speech group should make four or five impromptu talks during the course. I would suggest that as early as the second meeting some of these talks be worked in—as many as time permits—and that the time following the fifth and sixth talks, which are short, be devoted entirely to impromptus. The students get a lot out of these frequent brief appearances.

THE MECHANICS OF THE COURSE

Well before the first meeting, some member of the group should take over as temporary chairman, setting up the time and place for the first meeting and notifying the members. At the first meeting the group may elect a permanent chairman, decide to elect a chairman for each meeting, or decide to draw the chair by lot at each meeting. The duties of the chairman are to call the meeting to order, to announce the name of each speaker, to develop comments or discussion after each talk, to call for impromptu speeches when time permits, to assist the group in conducting any business, to have the group determine the time and place of the next meeting, to notify any absentee, to adjourn the meeting. This, of course, applies primarily to an independent study group. In a public school or college classroom, the mechanics are necessarily different and the teacher takes over as many of the chairman's functions as he or she thinks fit.

A simple way to set up the sequence of speakers is to have a piece of paper and pencil handy and as each person arrives at the meeting let him sign his name and the spot he wants in the "batting order." For instance, Tom Smith comes in first but decides he wants to speak third, so he signs "Tom Smith—3." The chairman then uses this list to announce each speaker.

You can schedule about six talks, five to six minutes in length, plus comments or impromptus, for every meeting hour. Therefore, if there are twelve people in the group, you might cover this course in a one-hour meeting (the first), plus seven two-hour meetings. If you adopt a schedule of this sort, there should be a short break in the middle of each two-hour meeting. In my opinion, a meeting much longer than that should not be attempted.

We need a word or two about the comments on the talks. To many Americans criticism means pointing out only the bad. Actually, I believe "review," or, in a sense, "analysis," is the truer meaning of the word—a pointing out of both the good and the bad. When we speak of criticizing a talk, that is what we mean. It is not a tearing down but rather a building up. A sensible idea, I believe, is for the chairman to ask after every talk, "What was good about this talk?" You can find some kind, constructive thing to say about every speaker and every talk, often easily, sometimes not, but you can find it. After the good things are brought out, the chairman should ask, "What could be improved?" Here, especially at the beginning of the course, limit the comment to one or two major mistakes, such as, let's say, not looking at the group. Don't smother the speaker with fifteen mistakes for him to correct next time. Let him concentrate on whatever big problem he has. When he beats that, then you can go on to the finer points. You are trying to be helpful, so, of course, the mean or sarcastic remark is particularly out of place.

Give as much honest praise as you can. As you may have noticed, I prefer to have all the talks made before there are any comments. The reason for this is that a beginning speaker is often, as the boys say, "shook up" right after his talk. He is not able to pay his best attention to the comments. He needs a cooling off period.

It is often helpful to the speaker to have each member of the group fill out a simple appraisal sheet. One like this can be made easily. Just circle the strong and weak points and add any comment.

Name			Talk No.		
Introduction	1	2	3	4	5
Central Idea or Purpose	1	2	3	4	5
Main Points	1	2	3	4	5
Support	1	2	3	4	5
Conclusion	1	2	3	4	5
Delivery	1	2	3	4	5

Comments

The course outlined above is also feasible, I believe, for a beginning Public Speaking class at any level—high school, prep school, or college. No matter how great a person's intellectual achievements, he remains a beginner in public speaking until he has made several talks before groups. The problems of all beginners are much the same and, I believe that, rather than start with a wide sweep of theory, the beginning Public Speaking course should be aimed directly at these problems. The purpose of this course should be simply to help every student learn to make a clear, interesting, effective little talk, and—the reverse of the coin—to help him learn to analyze why the other fellow is or isn't making an effective talk. To achieve this purpose, the student must develop confidence; he must master, not just become familiar with, but master, a hard core of essential theory; and he must be creative and determined enough to build half a dozen talks.

Because this book is written especially for the beginner and his problems, I believe it is an appropriate text for any beginning course in public speaking. I hope the student finds it both readable and instructive.